WILD!

JAMES CARTER is a poet and guitarist. He travels all over the UK and beyond to give lively poetry performances and workshops. He lives with a bunch of critters called Alice, Coco, Squidgy and Nibbles.

GRAHAM DENTON is a poet and anthologist who is absolutely wild about poetry for children. Graham dreams of one day going on an African safari, but for now is happy walking in the dales and woods near his East Yorkshire home, amongst the sheep, rabbits and pheasants, which, somewhat curiously, he often mistakes for cheetahs, giraffes and elephants.

Surrounded by many different species of birds, a gaggle of bears, a posse of pandas, the odd moose (including Uncle Sven in the attic) and strange pink things of indeterminate origin, JANE ECCLES finds plenty of inspiration for her illustrations. She still wants a dog though.

Also available from Macmillan

Time-Travelling Underpants
Poems by James Carter

There's a Hamster in the Fast Lane
Poems chosen by Brian Moses

The Jumble Book
Poems chosen by Roger Stevens

WILD!

Rhymes That Roar

Chosen by James Carter and Graham Denton

Illustrated by Jane Eccles

MACMILLAN CHILDREN'S BOOKS

First published 2009 by Macmillan Children's Books
a division of Macmillan Publishers Limited
20 New Wharf Road, London N1 9RR
Basingstoke and Oxford
www.panmacmillan.com

Associated companies throughout the world

ISBN: 978-0-330-46341-6

1 3 5 7 9 8 6 4 2

A CIP catalogue record for this book is available from
the British Library.

Printed and bound in the UK by CPI Mackays, Chatham ME5 8TD

For Simon and Kathy Donohoe (JC)

For Julie, Allan, Josh and Paige (GD)

For Theo, who loves all wildlife and birds (JE)

With big thanks to some fine
folk that are wild about wild things:
Gaby Morgan, James's dentist, and Jay Griffiths
for her inspirational masterpiece, WILD

Contents

Minibeasts

Amazing Mammals

Winged Things

Wild 'n' Wet

Reptiles and Amphibians

Welcome to Wild!

Ever been called a 'Wild Thing'? Or ever fancied escaping from it all, heading for the woods and living on nuts and berries? Well, now you don't have to. We've brought the wild to your very door! In this anthology you'll find poems, and a few facts too, which will hopefully give you a flavour of the 'wild' and some of the many weird and wonderful beasts that live within it.

So what does 'Wild' mean exactly? The undomesticated, the untamed, the uncivilized – anything out there that is natural. Or, in other words, anything that's not man-made. You share the Earth with the most marvellous, adaptable and intelligent creatures. That includes other humans. Yet you don't have to travel to the remotest parts of the planet just to witness wildlife at play. Wildness is all around us. Some quite remarkable life forms are acting out fantastic feats around your ears, beneath your feet and right in front of your eyes.

We knew early on that, while there was potential for a real breadth of material, *Wild!* could never be a 'definitive' modern collection of wildlife and nature poems for children.

There simply wasn't the room. There are literally millions of 'wild' animals in existence – over two million species have been identified to date. A book this size can only give voice to a fraction of those. With that in mind, we made an editorial decision to devote space to those creatures that are familiar and easily recognizable. But poetry allows us to see the familiar in new ways and in *Wild!* you'll find just that: poetry that paints original pictures, poetry that adds fresh colours to the canvas.

We wanted *Wild!* to be a collection of small celebrations. Some poems are thought-provoking; some are playful. But all have the X-factor that the natural world deserves.

So turn the page and go . . . wild!

Graham Denton and James Carter

GREEN THINGS

WILD!

Wild the garden overgrown
wild the jaw that breaks the bone

Wild the rain that soaks the sand
wild the sun that cracks the land

Wild the summer's green and greed
wild the wind that sows the seed

Wild the flower, big in bloom
wild the early dawning tune

Wild the bird that seeks the sun
wild the cry when life is done

Wild the claw that rips the skin
wild the bite, the tear, the sting

Wild the young that feed to grow
wild the blood that stains the snow

Wild the stench of fresh decay
wild the mulch that rots away

Wild the thorn, the fruit, the bud
wild the root, the shoot, the mud

Wild the song, the forest hum
wild the rhythm in the drum

Wild the honey in the comb
wild the hunter heading home

Wild the worm that breaks the soil
wild the world in constant toil

Wild the weed that lives in cracks
wild the scythe, the saw, the axe

Wild the heart at trees laid bare
wild the wild no longer there

James Carter

MAKING THE COUNTRYSIDE

Take a roll of green,
Spread it under a blue or blue-grey sky,
Hollow out a valley, mould hills.

Let a river run through the valley,
Let fish swim in it, let dippers
Slide along its surface.

Sprinkle cows in the water meadows,
Cover steep banks with trees,
Let foxes sleep beneath and owls above.

Now, let the seasons turn,
Let everything follow its course.
Let it be.

June Crebbin

A SMALL STAR

I live on a small star
Which it's my job to look after;
It whirls through space
Wrapped in a cloak of water.

It is a wonderful star:
Wherever you look there's life,
Though it's held at either end
In a white fist of ice.

There are creatures that move
Through air, sea and earth,
And growing things everywhere
Make beauty from dirt.

Everything is alive!
Even the stones:
Dazzling crystals grow
Deep under the ground.

And all the things belong,
Each one to the other.
I live on a precious star
Which it's my job to look after.

Gerard Benson

SOMETHING TO DO IN A TRAFFIC JAM

Dream of
a world where bat
and tiger wander free
and turtles set their courses by
the stars.

Judith Nicholls

WILDERNESS

Miss says wilderness
is beautiful, natural, endless . . .
is space.

Mum's Oxford English Dictionary states:
'wild or uncultivated land'.

At the end of our garden
there's a lime tree.
I climb it, high as I can.

Sometimes
I sit up there for hours,
especially in the dark
staring at the stars,
touching wilderness

out there
and inside me.

Joan Poulson

A MULTIPLICATION OF ONE

Nature started very small, as far we can tell,

beginning in the oceans as tiny single cells

and everything alive today arose from that one
source:

whale, giraffe and elephant, crocodile and
horse,

spider, shrimp and scorpion, crab, fly, fish and
flea

all had their origins in the vast primordial seas.

Frog and salamander, lizard, bird and bat,

kangaroo and human, monkey, badger, cat,

tree, grass, moss and flower, bacteria and mite

are branches of the same tree,

with all the world's delights

intertwined, connected, the tiny and the tall

each depending on the other, the greatest on
the small,

all springing from this one world, everything
from one,

on this blue-green planet beneath its friendly
sun.

Marian Swinger

THE TREES DANCE

Forest-father, mighty Oak:
On my back the lightning-stroke

Spear-maker, Ash-tree:
Safely cross the raging sea

Black-eyed Elder, crooked-arm:
Break me and you'll come to harm

Dark Yew, poison-cup:
Keep the ghosts from rising up

Summer's herald, Hawthorn, May:
Home of the fairies, keep away

Cry-a-leaf, the bitter Willow:
Where you walk at night I follow

Slender Hazel, water-hound:
In my nutshell wisdom found

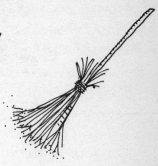

Birch the dancer, best broom:
Sweep the evil from your room

Fair Apple, fire's sweet wood:
Dreams of power and poets' food

Winter-shiner, Holly the king:
Good cheer to the cold I bring

Rowan the guard, berry-red:
Fairies fear and witches dread

Libby Houston

ANTHEM

Hawthorn-thick and nettle-deep
Place for nesting, resting, sleep,
Elder-frothed and bryony-bound
Sanctuary and breeding ground,
Flowering fence and living wall,
Rag-and-bobtail jumble stall –
Unsung hedgerow, thanks and praise
For your wild and secret ways.

Sue Cowling

FINDING MAGIC

Are you looking for magic?
It's everywhere.
See how a kestrel
Hovers in air;
Watch a cat move:
What elegant grace!
See how a conker
Fits its case.
Watch a butterfly come
From a chrysalis,
Or a chick from an egg –
There's magic in this;
Then think of the
Marvellous mystery
Of an acorn becoming
A huge oak tree.
There's magic in sunsets
And patterned skies:
There's magic in moonlight –
Just use your eyes!
If you're looking for magic
It's easily found:
It's everywhere,
It's all around.

Eric Finney

SEED SPELL

Bury me dark, bury me deep.
Let me lie awhile, asleep.

Let my root stretch out, uncoil,
sifting nurture from the soil.

Let me push my small shoot where
it reaches up to light and air.

Leaves uncrinkle, one by one,
soaking up bright rays of sun,

so that soil and light and air
help me grow, at last to bear

a flower that draws the fumbling bee
to store gold pollen at his knee . . .

and so the flower becomes a fruit
that holds a seed that grows a shoot

which, helped by soil and sun and rain,
begins the cycle once again,

as life goes slowly round and round
on Nature's strange, amazing ground.

Tony Mitton

ARE YOU
SLEEPWALKING?

Cats are more than alive.
That purposeful purr,
the ripple
of muscle and fur;
and bright eyes seen green
in midnight
headlights . . .

But what about trees?
They too grow slow,
stretching up;
their thin limbs
covered in rough skin.
They live and die.

But is water alive?
Like us it sleeps,
still and deep –
then shifts restlessly
like windblown silk,
or silver pouring from a tap.
If you touch water,
it moves aside,
its wet invitation
lets you slide in.

And rocks –
may be hard as nails,
but they wear a thin skin –
a cold crust of lichen;
icy in winter,
warmed by simple sun.
Like solid old men,
weathered till
they too crumble into dust.

You must look close enough,
to enter their world –
Even the grass seems alive –
as it uncurls its slim, green skin
and twists with the wind.

And what of you?
Have you yet woken to the world,
sensing its every move?
Or are you sleepwalking
through every waking moment?

Pie Corbett

BIG MOTHER

You don't get much more wild than me
and yet my child, we're family
but what I really ought to do
is introduce myself to you

I'm a gardener, that's my role
weeds to woods, I grow them all
celebrating every season
that's my life, my way, my reason

Listen now – beneath the ground:
hear that gentle rumbling sound?
There, that's me: I'm waiting, humming
my big summer gig is coming!

Love the damp, the dark, the night
love the wind, the heat, the light
but need the rain and need the sun –
help me grow up big and strong

Cut me down and I'll be back
crawling out through every crack
first a little dandelion
next a forest – I ain't lyin':

When I say I can't be tamed
I'm always there, but rarely named
I'll always win – and that I'll wager
I'm your other Mother – Nature

James Carter

Green Facts

Which Is False?

1. Like the human brain, seventy-five per cent of a living tree is water.

2. One single sandalwood tree in a forest can make a whole forest smell of sandalwood as the scent clings to other trees.

3. Ninety-nine per cent of the pumpkins sold in the United States end up as jack-o'-lanterns.

4. A fully grown oak tree sheds 250,000 leaves and 50,000 acorns.

5. The Jabberwocky tree in Lewis Carroll's poem of the same name is in the gardens of Christ Church, Oxford, and is over 3,000 years old.

Answer

5. Yes, the tree is in Oxford and did indeed inspire Lewis Carroll to write 'Jabberwocky', but the tree is actually only a few hundred years old.

22

MINIBEASTS

BUG HUG

Hey
little
bug – how
do you hug –
or cuddle or kiss
your mum or sis –
with all those arms
and legs and things –
and wiggly bits and
wobbly wings? For
however hairy or
creepy or scary
even the ugliest
bug needs
a HUG!

gimme a hug! *gimme a hug!*

gimme a hug! *gimme a hug!*

gimme a hug! *gimme a hug!*

James Carter

MOSQUITO

This vampire flyer
Has one desire:
To dip its
Straw
into
yo-
u r
p
o r
e
!

Robert Scotellaro

BEES

Every bee
that
ever was
was
partly
sting
and partly
. . . buzz.

Jack Prelutsky

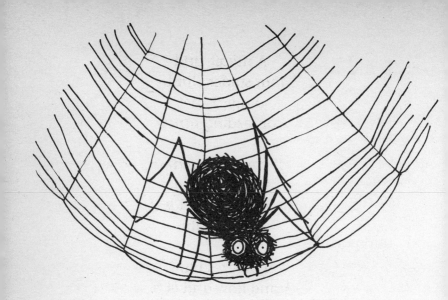

SPIDER'S WEB

Spider's web
is spider's home
is spider's world
that spider's grown

Spider's web
is spider's skill
at spinning circles
in a wheel

Spider weaves
the sticky thread
and makes a giant
magic bed

A magic grid
that spider climbs
a magic net
for feeding times

If creature breaks
the magic frame
then spider builds it
back again

If breezes blow
bring flow and ebb
then spider clings
to spider's web

And spun with tender
loving care –
finest palace
anywhere

James Carter

HAIKU RIDDLE BUGS

1. Menace to greenfly,
   A small, round, red domino,
   Flying away home.

2. Silently he climbs
   2, 4, 6, 8 legs, clinging –
   Soon the scream will come!

3. Full of leaves, at rest.
   Camping in a silken tent,
   Waiting for rebirth.

4. Shiny black armour
   with a taste for leftovers!
   Humming through the air.

5. Wriggling and wiggling:
   A problem in the kitchen,
   A fisherman's friend.

Coral Rumble

Answers

1. Ladybird, 2. Spider, 3. Caterpillar, 4. Dung beetle, 5. Maggot

28

BEAST

Doyen of the dead night. Silent goth.
Bullet-bodied babe of light-lured wrath.
Spell-born grub-spawn from a witchcraft broth.

Papery wings of powdery cloth
Dyed the dark hues of the cauldron's froth.
Shadow of a butterfly. Fluttering moth.

Nick Toczek

29

WHAT'S A CATERPILLAR?

Little
but a fly
in waiting.

Graham Denton

COCKROACH

Scuttle-bug,
shadow-foot,
bringer of night;
sky without stars,
obsidian-light;
shiny as coal,
new-mined and still bright;
smooth as new carbon,
dark and untyped.

Judith Nicholls

Bug Facts

Which Is False?

1. Butterflies eat through their feet.

2. A flea can jump 350 times its body length, which is like a human jumping the length of a football field.

3. The ant can lift fifty times its own weight, and can pull thirty times its own weight.

4. Slugs have four noses and 3,000 teeth.

5. Mosquitoes bite.

Answer

5. Oh no they don't! They actually stab you. A mosquito pierces you with its proboscis and then sucks up the blood through it. Charming!

HIPPO

oh!
hippo
pot
amus!
happy hippo
smiling, sinking,
deep in the cool
of your muddy pool
making
your back
like an island
in a brown river.

Ann Bonner

WHO'S THIS?

Slow - mover
floe - walker
stealth - hunter
seal - stalker

Ice - gripper
sharp - clawer
den - digger
loud - roarer

Keen - smeller
storm - beater
north - poler
lone - creature

Thick - coater
cold - lover
big - footer
snow - brother

Of all the living
quadrupeds,
who's this
avalanche on legs?

Graham Denton

Answer
Polar bear

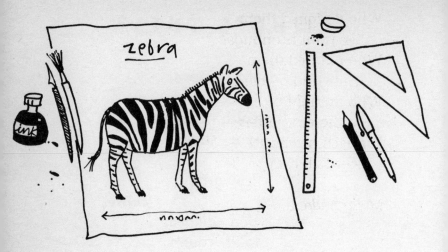

ZEBRA

Who let them loose
  with face paints?
Who gave them pyjamas
  to wear?
Who made them look
  like newspapers?
Who striped them
  here and there?

Who designed them
   like mint humbugs?
Who painted them
   white and black?
Who thought of
   a different pattern
For each newborn
   zebra's back?

Moira Andrew

LION

Great ragbag
jumble-headed thing
shakes its mane
in a yawn that turns to anger,
teeth picked out like stalactites
in some vast cave
bone-grinders, flesh-rippers
hyena bringers, jackal callers
and huge paws
the size of death
clamp down on antelope,
later, sleeping through the night
each star a lion
flung with pride across a sky
black as a roaring mouth
lion dreams of open spaces
dreams the smell of freedom.

David Harmer

TIGER

When the tiger roars
        look! he grows a mouth so wide
                it swallows his eyes

Graham Denton

MONKEY

I am
swing-on-a-tail,
up with the sun
fast as white lightning
slits skies at noon.
Now under palms,
now over fern;
dawn-creeper, branch-leaper,
dive, twist and turn.
Face-in-the-forest,
chasing the moon;
tree-lover, sky-brother,
dew-dancing one.

Judith Nicholls

37

ELEPHANTS

They come in a dusty mass,
these gentle giants of the waterhole,
lumbering into the brown shallows
to cool their massive feet.

They sluice up water with fire-hose
trunks into parched throats,
shrug weariness
out of their wrinkled hides.

That done, they sway deeper,
roll ecstatically in mud.
Lazily, they shower off
the heat of the day's trek.

The calves splash, tug, tumble,
play water fights while mothers,
sisters, grandmothers
flick ears and look on.

Games over,
the grandmother of all mothers
shakes her frame, turns tail
and leads them towards shade.

They merge into the wood and leaves,
shadows within grey shadows.
They close up, nuzzle each other,
and small eyes droop.

Some, wise with old memories,
keep watch.

Patricia Leighton

(*Elephant herds are made up of females and young calves, with one of the older females as leader. These family groups are very close and protective. The male calves will go off to live in small 'teenage groups', and later alone, only linking up with the herd again for mating.*)

GORILLA GAZING
(London Zoo – Easter 2008)

He sits and he stares
with them old brown eyes
beyond the glass
beyond my gaze
to a time
and a place
he's never known
yet somehow
seems to remember

Where the wind
shakes the trees
where the rain
wets the leaves
where there are
no walls at all

He sits and he stares
like an ancient sage
beyond the glass
beyond my gaze
to a world
long gone
and wonders why
we're all
so far
from home

James Carter

THE WOLF OUTSIDE

I wake.   I know.
No need   to see.
A visitor has come for me. That
wolf is at the door again. In the
dark, the pouring rain. He makes
no sound – he needs to hear my
breath, my pulse, my thoughts,
my fear. We wait together. Two
souls still. I need to live, he
needs to kill. He leaves. I
breathe. I sigh and how.
I check. The wolf
has gone,
for now.

James Carter

THE BEAR BELOW

I'm sat
high in an ancient
tree – the bear below peers
up at me . . . He can't climb up,
I can't come down – and so we
simply hang around . . . He pads
about, he whacks the tree – he sniffs
the air, he glares at me. He growls,
he prowls, he bares his teeth –
he rubs his fur . . . he goes to
sleep. Then quiet, calm –
till something
stirs –
now
here's
a wolf . . .
can things
get worse?!?

James Carter

THE BROWN BEAR

In the dark wood
In a clearing
Sleeps a brown bear
Dreaming, dreaming

His skin is furless
His paws are clawless
He walks into the city
Lawless, lawless

The moon is hidden
The clouds are weeping
A princess slumbers
Sleeping, sleeping

The thief creeps through
The royal bedroom
And steals her ruby
A priceless heirloom

The ruby glows
With fire and lightning
A spell is cast
So frightening, frightening

The thief grows fur
His body thickens
His hands grow claws
He sickens, sickens

Beneath the black sky
Thunder rumbles
Into the dark wood
He stumbles, stumbles

For in the ruby
Gleaming, gleaming
A wizard's mind
Is scheming, scheming

Now, in the dark wood
In a clearing
Sleeps a brown bear
Dreaming, dreaming

Roger Stevens

MOUSE LAUGHING

Have you ever heard Mouse laughing?
You'd be surprised.
It doesn't sound as you'd suppose.
No it doesn't.
No squeaks, no twitterings,
No pussyfooting around.
More of a belly laugh, really.
Like the trumpeting howl of an elephant
Thudding across the parched plains of Africa,
Or the deep-throated rumble of the earth
At its centre.
You needn't believe me, of course.
But next time you meet Mouse,
Don't tickle him.

Mary Green

SIX O'CLOCK FOX

Cop-
per coat
ablaze, tail brushing stubble, he stalks,
pauses . . . picking paws he pricks signal ears,
directs wet pebble eyes beyond his
twitch of whiskers. Freeze-framed, he
holds   the moment,   then sweeps
to   streak   towards
the   swell
-ing   sun.

Gina Douthwaite

Mammal Facts

Which Is False?

1. Elephants really are afraid of mice.

2. Polar bears are left-handed.

3. A mole can dig a tunnel a hundred metres long in just one night.

4. Foxes steal hens' eggs by carrying them with their teeth – and then often go off and bury them fifteen centimetres under the ground for the time when food is scarce.

5. There are 900 different types of bat. The smallest – the very rare bumblebee bat – is also the smallest mammal. AND bats always turn left when leaving a cave.

Answer

1. No they're not! Elephants are so high up they don't even notice mice!

48

WINGED THINGS

PARROT

Parrot flames on his branch;
his beak is a battleaxe.

His encircled eye
pierces what it sees.

He screams like a soprano;
moves among the leaves like a rock climber.

He dazzles the forest canopy
with primary colours. A celebration.

Gerard Benson

49

FIVE HAIKU FOR THE BIRDS

Robin   Flashing your red badge
          You fix me with a bold eye:
          Christmas-card hunchback.

Buzzard   There against the blue,
          A nonchalant skymaster
          Riding the thermals.

Wren   Wee bird, hardly seen –

          Just a flicker in the hedge.
          Jaunty though, that tail.

Goldfinch   Such colours! You bring
To a dull December day
A tropical touch.

Rooks   High in wintry trees
In cawing conversation:
Swirling torn black rags.

Eric Finney

MYNAH PROBLEMS

The mynah bird
has quite a gimmick –
you'll find that there's
no finer mimic.
I've heard, if taught,
one of these birds
can learn up to
a hundred words.
But, as it mocks the
things it hears,
be careful what goes
in its ears;
a mynah's quick
to pick up speech
you likely didn't
mean to teach,
which they then go
about repeating . . .
and make you wish they'd
stick to tweeting.

Graham Denton

HUMMINGBIRD

Hummingbird,   hummingbird,
    Amazing as   a magic word.
        Rainbows flash out
       From your wings.
        The sweet air
        Through
        your
        feathers
        sings
        !

Jan Dean

BARN OWL

Silent as moonlight,
snowy-white hunter
waits in a high branch,
hungry as winter.

Still as the North Star,
patiently watching,
eyes black as nightfall,
claws curved and clutching.

Fast as an arrow
shot from a quiver,
back in the treetops,
blood on white feathers.

Silent as moonlight,
snowy-white hunter
waits in a high branch,
hungry as winter.

Celia Gentles

CROW

You will have noticed me
Swooping down, hoarsely calling –
A black, oiled sheen of bird.
I dodge telephone wires, skim chimney corners,
Perch on rooftop angles and circle over
    playgrounds.

My business is theft – eggs, fledglings.
I am without conscience,
My mind is as sharp as hooked claws.
I believe in a pecking order,
Survival of the quickest.
Nothing wrong with being an opportunist,
A scavenger, raider, cruel invader.
My reputation hangs on a cloak of terror.

Coral Rumble

Feathered Facts

Which Is False?

1. A chicken which has just lost its head (oh yuck!) can run the length of a football field before dropping dead.

2. A group of crows is called a murder.

3. A hummingbird weighs less than a penny.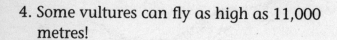

4. Some vultures can fly as high as 11,000 metres!

5. Emperor penguins can stay underwater for several hours.

Answer

5. No way, matey! Penguins don't have gills or diving gear! The maximum dive time for an emperor penguin is eighteen minutes.

56

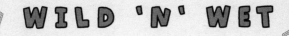

WILD 'N' WET

chomp
Chomp

EEL-ECTRIC!

You wouldn't think electric eels
Were given to excessive meals,
But yes, indeed, they're greedy eaters –
I guess they need to feed their meters.

Graham Denton

IT'S WHERE?

It's where mermaids call their home
it's where pirates used to roam
It's where penguins have their tea
it's where people like to be

It's deep it's damp it's big it's blue
it's green it's grey it's turquoise too
It's freezing cold and wild and yet
it could be called the world wide wet

It's where baby clouds are made
it's where children love to bathe
It's where toddlers often wee
to you and me it's called . . . the sea

James Carter

OCTO-PUZZLE

This boneless bandit
of the sea
strangle-wraps
his enemy.
Lazy lobsters are
his bait.
His wild *army*
numbers
eight.

Rebecca Kai Dotlich

OYSTER

Miraculously turning
grit into lustrous pearls:
oyster magic

Cynthia Rider

ROCK POOL

Down there,
peer – if you dare –
hidden in the seaweed strands,
things are scuttling, sifting soft sand.
Beware!

Mike Johnson

WHALE MUSIC

Great underwater Zeppelin,
sea-salt singer,
hoovering up
the soupy oceans,
the minestrone waves!

When I first heard
your thar-she-blows,
your old grampus
huffing and puffing,

I thought you were
some enormous sea horse
snorting . . .

and when I saw
your tail-flukes flop
and plunge

I thought you were
a huge black angel
falling into the ocean . . .

O submarine gargler,
I have listened
to your sad, mysterious songs,
your clickings
and crooning
fathoms down

and wished
there was a way
of singing songs
to you.

Matt Simpson

THE AXOLOTL

You are the Peter Pan
Of the silent world
Where secret rivers flow
Through hidden caves,
And sinister rocks stare
With hollow eyes.

You flutter the pale wings
Of your gills
And gaze at your own
Neverland,
While bats rise like lost children
And stalagmites loom
Like the sails of tall ships.

Brave axolotl
With your eyes full of dreams,
I wish I could be like you
And never grow up,
Never grow up.

Clare Bevan

(An axolotl is a salamander that never becomes an adult.)

LOBSTER

Inside my slaty shell, blue-black as ink
I sink into green water.
Armoured like a knight
With spike and saw of crack-bone claw
I choose not to fight –
Prefer the quiet of holes,
The sea shadow of tall rocks
Where flocks of fish and shrimp shoals
Shiver pale and silver on slivers of stone.
In here I hunch,
Curl the crunch of my tough tail
Beneath me.
Stay still, unobserved,
Only my long antennae
Silently taste the moving tides
Receive the salty messages
Of the dark and secret sea.

Jan Dean

THE DIVERS
AND THE DOLPHINS

Ah, just look at them,
aren't they beautiful?

So graceful, so sleek
as they swim around the boat –

poking their snouts up
to break the surface,

then diving straight down,
blowing bubbles all the time.

And look at all their different colours.
I'll bet they could fetch things.

I've even seen one
dive deep down to a wrecked ship.

Look at its oval eye, so large, so glassy.
And listen; I'm sure they're communicating.

Not 'talking' as we know it,
but they're certainly intelligent.

Strange how those land-leggers feel they have
to dive underwater from time to time.

John Rice

HAIKU

The great white shark's teeth –
     three thousand tombstones in the
graveyard of a mouth

Graham Denton

Sea Facts

Which Is False?

1. Starfish do not have brains.

2. A fish has a memory span of three seconds.

3. A catfish has twenty-seven taste buds.

4. A blue whale's heart only beats nine times per minute.

5. A female mackerel lays about 500,000 eggs at one time.

Answer

3. A catfish has 27,000 taste buds – more than any other creature in the world.

REPTILES AND AMPHIBIANS

LUNCHTIME
FOR LIZARDS

insect
    o
      n
        g
          u
            e
                CHAMELEON
                    m
                    m
                    m
                    m
                    m
                    m
                    !

Mike Johnson

70

FROGS

frog chorus . . .
under every chin
a moon resonating

Carol Coiffait

VISIBLE INVISIBLE
(haiku)

In and out of sight
the sandy sidewinder slides:
now you see him, now . . .

Kate Williams

CROCODILES!

Crocodiles

are **R**eally cunning fighters.

With m**O**nstrous jaws

and **C**rushing teeth

they're awes**O**me biters.

Like **D**ead tree trunks

they float **I**n swamps,

waiting for **L**unch.

Then they'll sudd**E**nly attack.

Snap! Crunch!

Wes Magee

TURTLE BEACH

In the quiet of the evening
When the beach is long deserted,
While the moon is shining brightly
And the sand lies softly dreaming,
Under cover of the darkness
See the coming of the turtles,
Leaving their familiar waters,
Crawling up the beach in hundreds,
Digging holes above the tideline,
Flippers delving ever deeper,
Gently nesting in the moonlight,
Laying eggs in secret chambers.
Then the turtle mothers turning
Haul their heavy bodies seaward,
Back towards the pounding breakers
And the comfort of the ocean.

Sue Cowling

THIS OLD TORTOISE

They say,
This old tortoise can remember:
Top hats and crinolines,
Airships and omnibuses,
Suffragettes and soldiers,
Flappers and silent films,
Sirens and doodlebugs,
Mickey Mouse gas masks
And children on steam trains,
Coronations and street parties,
Beatles and flower power,
Spaceships and moon dust,
Computers and pop stars,
Harry Potter and hurricanes,
Comets and eclipses . . .

But I say,
This old tortoise can remember:
Lettuce and celery,
Carrots and cabbage leaves,
Sunshine and showers,
More lettuce and endless lawns
Of sweet, wet grass.

Clare Bevan

SO SMALL?

and now someone has seen
the teeniest lizard there's ever been
in existence, a gecko smaller
than my baby sister's finger

and I'm wondering
if somewhere there could be
herds of tiny elephants,
giraffes and hippopotami browsing

a grassy clearing in a forest
where sunlight washes over a splash
of green water and on the edge
thumb-size crocodiles snooze

while among the plants and shrubs
mini-geckos flicker elastic tongues,
catch flies that cloud the air
like specks of dust.

Joan Poulson

HAIKU MOMENTS

A frog's bulging eyes
gaze glassily at a bug.
The bug vanishes.

Quicksilver lizards
dart across a rotten log,
tongues tasting the air.

An idle adder
basks on a sun-soaked sandbank.
Beetle skitters past. . . . .

A great crested newt
hangs, suspended in water
like a small dragon.

A toad in peril
puffs up like a small balloon.
Enemy retreats.

A slow-worm's shed tail
squirms on a hot garden path.
A cat squints at it.

Wriggling black commas
clinging to ragged frogspawn.
Predators gather.

Beneath the water,
a dark and sinuous shape.
A grass snake hunting.

Marian Swinger

KOMODO DRAGON

Here be creatures
    ten feet long
Here be beasts
    immense and strong
Here be huge
    and brawny tails
Here be skin
    with brownish scales

Here be brutes
    who overpower
Here be monsters
    that devour
Here be jaws
    with lethal bites
Here be giant
    appetites

Here be kings
    from days of old
Here be tales
    the ancients told
Here be teeth
    of dinosaurs
Here be feet
    with razor claws

Here be foul
  and fetid breath
Here be eyes
  as cold as death
Here be legends
  newly born
Here be dragons . . .
  you've been warned!

Graham Denton

(*The world's largest living lizard, the Komodo dragon or monitor lizard, is found only on Komodo, Indonesia, and its few smaller outlying islands. It has probably only ever lived in this small area, although maps made by ancient mariners had notations of 'here be dragons' marked on islands dotted across what is now Malaysia and Indonesia. It was not until the early 1900s that scientists confirmed the existence of these incredible giant reptiles.*)

LIZARDS

Slick little
        quick little
sleek little
        meek little
lizard
    with scales on
your skin –
   darting
and hurrying
        turning
and scurrying
        briskly
now out
    and now in.

Stone cracks
　　and crevices
dark
　　and mysterious
keep you
　　　in coolness
and night
　　　　till the sun
quickens you
　　　　with a long
finger, to
　lure you out
into
　　the light.

Jean Kenward

Reptile and Amphibian Facts

Which Is False?

1. A crocodile cannot stick its tongue out.

2. Hundreds of millions of years ago, amphibians became the first vertebrates to live on land.

3. Some turtles and tortoises, including the Eastern box turtle, can live for more than five thousand years.

4. Depending upon the size of the meal, anacondas can go several months between each one.

5. Australia has a plague of cane toads – 100 million of them to be precise.

Answer

3. Well, actually, if they are lucky, they'll live for over a hundred years.

A selected list of titles available from Macmillan Children's Books

The prices shown below are correct at the time of going to press. However, Macmillan Publishers reserves the right to show new retail prices on covers, which may differ from those previously advertised.

Laugh Out Loud	978-0-330-45456-8	**£4.99**
Chosen by Fiona Waters		
I'd Rather Be a Footballer	978-0-330-45713-2	**£4.99**
Paul Cookson		
I Had a Little Cat –		
Collected Poems for Children	978-0-330-46865-7	**£6.99**
Charles Causley		

All Pan Macmillan titles can be ordered from our website, www.panmacmillan.com, or from your local bookshop and are also available by post from:

Bookpost, PO Box 29, Douglas, Isle of Man IM99 1BQ

Credit cards accepted. For details:
Telephone: 01624 677237
Fax: 01624 670923
Email: bookshop@enterprise.net
www.bookpost.co.uk

Free postage and packing in the United Kingdom